A WORLD AFTER . . .

an
ASTEROID
STRIKE

Alex Woolf

Heinemann
LIBRARY

Chicago, Illinois

Edited by Andrew Farrow, Adrian Vigliano,
  and Vaarunika Dharmapala
Designed by Philippa Jenkins
Original illustrations © Capstone Global Library
  Limited 2013
Illustrated by HL Studios and Alvaro Fernandez
  Villa Advocate-Art pp4-5
Picture research by Mica Brancic
Printed and bound in China

17 16 15 14 13
10 9 8 7 6 5 4 3 2 1

**Library of Congress Cataloging-in-
Publication Data**
Woolf, Alex, 1964-
  An asteroid strike / Alex Woolf.—1st ed.
    p. cm.—(A world after)
  Includes bibliographical references and
index.
  ISBN 978-1-4329-7618-7 (hb)—ISBN 978-1-
4329-7623-1 (pb)
1. Asteroids—Collisions with Earth—Environ-
mental aspects—Juvenile literature. 2. Catas-
trophes (Geology)—Juvenile literature. I. Title.

  QB651.W66 2013
  363.3'49—dc23   2012034743

Acknowledgments
We would like to thank the following for
permission to reproduce photographs: Alamy
pp 28 (© David Noton Photography/David Noton), 32 (© Frontline Pictures), 43 (© Jeff Mor-
gan 14); Corbis pp 7 (epa/© Terje Bendiksby/),
17 (epa/© Terje Bendiksby/), 30 (Demotix/Al-
bert Gonzalez Farran), 31 (Demotix/© M- Kol-
lective/), 37 (© Sam Diephuis); Getty Images
pp 10 inset (NASA), 14 (Martin Hunter), 19
(AFP), 22 (AFP Photo/Natalia Kolesnikova), 23
(Robert Nickelsberg), 24 (Oxford Scientific), 38
(Oli Scarff), 41 (Foto24/Gallo Images); NASA p
36 (Goddard/SDO AIA Team); Photoshot p 11;
Rex Features pp 6, 21 (Everett/TM & copyright
20th Century Fox); Science Photo Library p 46
(Detlev Van Ravenswaay); The Kobal Collection
p 20 (Frank Masi/Dreamworks/Paramount);
The Spaceguard Centre & Observatory p 45
(Jay Tate); Xome Arquitectos p 39.

Design features throughout courtesy of
Shutterstock: empty cork bulletin board,
background (© Reinhold Leitner), storm
clouds (© KavardakovA), chain link fence
(© ARENA Creative).

Cover photograph of the Statue of
Liberty against an apocalyptic background
reproduced with permission of Shutterstock
(© olly).

In creating the scenario of an asteroid strike
for this book, the author was particularly
helped by two papers: "Comet and Asteroid
Threat Impact Analysis" by James A. Marusek
(American Institute of Aeronautics and
Astronautics, 2007) and "Asteroid Impact
Tsunami of 2880, March 16" by Steven N. Ward
and Erik Asphaug (Geophysical Journal
International, 2003).

We would like to thank Paul Roche for his
invaluable help in the preparation of this book.

Disclaimer

CONTENTS

Some words are printed in bold, **like this**. You can find out
what they mean by looking in the glossary.

Friday, April 6, 2020. Some friends are walking along a beach on a Caribbean island. It is a warm evening. A faint breeze stirs the mangrove trees. Meanwhile, over 1,200 miles (2,000 kilometers) above their heads, a giant rock is speeding through the void on a collision course with Earth...

This is the life.

So much nicer than home.

Warm tonight, isn't it?

Wh-What was that?

Quick, let's get to the ocean.

I'm burning!

THREAT FROM THE SKIES

When we look up at the sky at night, the universe seems like a peaceful place. Actually, it is incredibly violent up there. Most of the really dangerous things, such as exploding stars and black holes that suck in everything around them, are too far away to threaten us. But that doesn't mean it is safe or peaceful in our corner of the universe. Rocks hurtle their way through our solar system at speeds of up to 93,200 miles (150,000 kilometers) per hour. Like Earth, they are in orbit around the Sun. The vast majority of these rocks will not come near us, but some of them will—and some of them will hit us.

Frequent strikes

In fact, we get hit by rocks from space more often than you might think. Each year, several thousand of these rocks, known as **meteoroids**, strike Earth's surface. Meteoroids are small—less than 33 feet (10 meters) in diameter— so they do not do much damage. But very occasionally, we get hit by bigger objects, known as asteroids or comets, and these can do a lot of damage. In this book, we are going to look at what might happen if Earth got struck by a very big asteroid—one that was over half a mile (1 kilometer) wide! As you will see, this would be very bad news for the whole planet.

↗ This image shows the trail of one of the meteorites that fell in Russia on February 15, 2013.

People didn't always believe that we were getting hit by rocks from space. In 1807, U.S. President Thomas Jefferson said:

"I would more easily believe that a Yankee professor would lie than that stones would fall from heaven."

The president said this in response to Professor Benjamin Silliman of Yale University, who claimed that a rock had fallen from the sky in Weston, Connecticut. It wasn't until the 1830s that people began to accept the existence of meteoroids.

But don't worry too much. Asteroids of this size strike Earth extremely rarely—around once every 600,000 years. Astronomers scan the skies for large rocks heading our way, so hopefully we will get plenty of warning. We might even be able to send up a spacecraft to deflect the asteroid away from Earth (see page 46). Now, let's take a closer look at these different types of space rock.

Meteoroids

Meteoroids are the smallest kind of **extraterrestrial** rock. They can be anything from a grain of space dust to a large boulder. Like Earth, meteoroids orbit the Sun. They are made of stone or metal, and most come from asteroids that have been shattered by hitting other asteroids. Other meteoroids come from comets, the Moon, or Mars.

More than 40,000 tons of meteoroids enter Earth's atmosphere every year, though only a few thousand small pieces make it to the surface. Most of them burn up when they hit Earth's atmosphere. When a meteoroid enters the atmosphere, the air in front of it compresses very quickly, causing the temperature to rise. The meteoroid heats up and starts to glow. This trail of light, which you can sometimes see in the night sky, is called a **meteor**, or shooting star. The meteoroids that actually reach Earth's surface are known as **meteorites**.

These are fragments of a possible meteorite that hit the roof of a cottage in Oslo, Norway, in March 2012.

Asteroids

Asteroids are rocky or metallic objects that range from 33 feet (10 meters) across to several hundred miles across. Astronomers think they are debris left over from the formation of the solar system—the remains of objects that failed to become planets. Most asteroids orbit in the "asteroid belt" between the orbits of Mars and Jupiter. However, asteroids are found all over the solar system, including near Earth.

Asteroids are affected by the gravitational pull of larger objects such as planets, and they can be pulled out of their orbits and become a planet's satellite. The moons of Mars—Phobos and Deimos—may be former asteroids. Astronomers think that if the giant planet Jupiter did not exert such a powerful gravitational force, asteroids would be constantly bombarding the inner planets, including Earth. So, we may have Jupiter to thank for not experiencing more asteroid strikes here on Earth!

COMETS

Comets are balls of ice, dust, and gas. When close to the Sun, they display long tails. These are formed when the Sun melts the ice in the comet, releasing lots of dust and gas. Solar winds push this dust and gas away from the comet to create the tail. These tails can reach up to 93 million miles (150 million kilometers) in length!

Each time a comet passes near the Sun, it loses some material. Over time, it will break up and disappear completely—if it does not collide with another celestial body first! Comets have collided with Earth in the distant past. Most scientists think a large fraction of Earth's water may have been delivered by comet impacts shortly after the planet formed.

Craters

Scientists have estimated that over the past 600 million years, Earth has been struck by 60 objects of 3 miles (5 kilometers) diameter or more. How do we know this? Well, when asteroids strike Earth, they leave a crater. Many of these craters have been found. The largest of these include Vredefort Crater in South Africa, Chicxulub Crater in Mexico, and Manicouagan and Sudbury Craters in Canada.

HOW LIKELY IS IT?

How likely is it that a giant asteroid could hit Earth?

The following table shows the average length of time between asteroid strikes of various sizes, as well as their possible effects. As you can see, the larger the asteroid, the rarer the strike.

Diameter (feet)	Average interval between impacts (years)	Energy release (**megatons TNT**)	Crater diameter (miles)
100	200	2	0
165	2,500	10	about 0.5
330	5,000	80	over 1
650	47,000	600	2.5
1,650	200,000	10,000	over 6
3,300	600,000	80,000	over 12
16,400	20 million	10 million	over 60
32,800	100 million	80 million	125

The iridium layer

Geologists have also found other evidence of asteroid strikes. In 1980, high concentrations of the element iridium were found in a layer of rock in Earth's crust. Iridium is rare on the surface of Earth, but it is found in asteroids. Further discoveries of this iridium layer were soon being made all over the world. In the same layer, they found large amounts of soot, ash, and shocked quartz. Shocked quartz is a mineral formed under extremely high pressures. It is found only at nuclear bomb test sites and in impact craters. From this, some geologists concluded that an asteroid of 6 to 13 miles (10 to 20 kilometers) diameter struck Earth around 65 million years ago.

The death of dinosaurs

This coincides with the time when dinosaurs and many other plant and animal species were wiped out. Long before the iridium layer was discovered, scientists had pondered the reasons for this so-called "mass extinction event," meaning many species died out. Now, perhaps, the mystery had been solved. Perhaps the impact of the enormous asteroid shook up Earth's climate so much that it caused thousands of species to die out—including the dinosaurs (see box on page 10).

Impact winter

How could an asteroid striking one part of Earth change the climate of the entire planet? Scientists have calculated that the impact of a large asteroid would send up huge amounts of dust into Earth's atmosphere. The energy and heat produced by the impact could also spark enormous fires in Earth's forested areas, adding smoke and ash to the dust in the atmosphere. All this smoke, ash, and dust would circulate around the globe, blocking the Sun's light. Temperatures would drop, causing an "impact winter." Plants would struggle to grow in these conditions and animals would starve.

In addition to having long-term effects on Earth's climate, asteroids also have an immediate effect on the area where they fall. The impact of an asteroid releases huge amounts of energy. Objects with diameters of 16 to 33 feet (5 to 10 meters) enter Earth's atmosphere about once a year and explode with about the same energy as the atomic bomb dropped on Hiroshima, Japan, in 1945. Most of these explode in the upper atmosphere.

CHICXULUB CRATER

Many scientists think that a giant asteroid wiped out the dinosaurs. But where did it land? The most likely site is the Chicxulub Crater in the Yucatán Peninsula, Mexico, which was created 65 million years ago. The crater is more than 110 miles (180 kilometers) in diameter, and scientists estimate the asteroid must have struck with a force equivalent to over 100 million megatons of TNT—which is two million times more powerful than the biggest nuclear bomb ever detonated!

Russian meteors

On February 15, 2013, a meteor exploded over Chelyabinsk province in southern Russia. The explosion took place 9–15 miles (15–25 kilometers) above the ground and was 20–30 times more powerful than the Hiroshima atomic bomb. Nearly 1,500 people were injured, mainly from shattered glass. Up to 3,000 buildings in six cities received damage. Eyewitnesses reported seeing a dazzling light in the sky, bright enough to cast shadows. Many felt an intense heat from the fireball. The meteor is the largest object known to have entered Earth's atmosphere since the 1908 Tunguska event, and the only one to have caused large-scale injuries.

The "Tunguska Event" of 1908 was an explosion about 3 or 6 miles (5 or 10 kilometers) above Earth's surface, caused by an asteroid or comet fragment of around 100 to 130 feet (30 to 40 meters) in diameter. The event took place over the Podkamennaya Tunguska River in Russia. Around 80 million trees were knocked over by the event.

IMPACT! THE FIRST FEW HOURS

At 6:15 p.m. **Eastern Standard Time** on Friday, April 6, 2020, an asteroid of approximately 3,600 feet (1,100 meters) diameter strikes Earth. Traveling at 11 miles (18 kilometers) per second, it smashes into the North Atlantic Ocean about 375 miles (600 kilometers) east of the coast of the United States. The impact generates a 60,000 megaton blast, vaporizing the asteroid and blowing a cavity in the ocean that is 12 miles (19 kilometers) across and 3 miles (5 kilometers) deep. It even makes a crater in the ocean floor.

How did such a massive object escape the notice of Earth's space-based asteroid monitoring systems? Unfortunately, the object was dark and approached from a sunward direction, making it difficult to observe. Also, this was a sector of the sky that was not being closely watched at the time, due to cuts in the funding of space research.

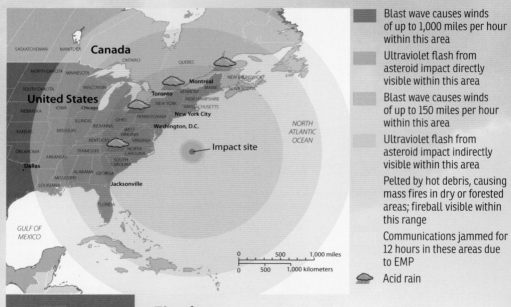

Blast wave causes winds of up to 1,000 miles per hour within this area

Ultraviolet flash from asteroid impact directly visible within this area

Blast wave causes winds of up to 150 miles per hour within this area

Ultraviolet flash from asteroid impact indirectly visible within this area

Pelted by hot debris, causing mass fires in dry or forested areas; fireball visible within this range

Communications jammed for 12 hours in these areas due to EMP

Acid rain

This is the area of the North Atlantic Ocean where the asteroid lands.

Flash

The first thing anyone notices is a flash of light. As the asteroid enters the atmosphere, it produces intense ultraviolet light, many times brighter than the Sun. The flash lasts millionths of a second, but eight people who happen to be looking directly at it—three aboard American Airlines Flight 714 and five aboard the cruise ship MS *Limburg*—suffer permanent damage to their eyes. The flash is indirectly visible to people up to 870 miles (1,400 kilometers) away. Many of those exposed to it suffer temporary **flash blindness**.

Electromagnetic effects

The second noticeable effect of the impact is an **electromagnetic pulse (EMP)**. This is a burst of **electromagnetic radiation** caused by high-energy explosions, such as nuclear explosions or, as in this case, an asteroid impact. The EMP does not harm humans, but it creates a violent **electric current** surge that is highly damaging to electronics. Every village, town, and city within 1,550 miles (2,500 kilometers) of the impact zone suffers an immediate power failure. It will be hours before power in many places is restored.

At the same time, the impact produces large amounts of **ionizing radiation**. This is a form of radiation that can strip electrons from atoms or molecules, producing ions—atoms or molecules with an electric charge. The ionizing radiation disrupts electromagnetic waves passing through the upper atmosphere, causing a significant interruption to communication signals. Across the world, telephones, televisions, computers, and radios temporarily stop working. The Internet shuts down, and for the next few hours, global communications virtually cease, seriously hampering the first rescue efforts.

Even areas not affected by the EMP witness a sudden increase in telephone and Internet traffic, as people try to find out what just happened and check that their loved ones are okay. This surge in communications overwhelms many networks.

The EMP also disables a number of satellites, causing the temporary loss of GPS navigation and the crash of the global banking system.

FACT OR FICTION?

A flaming streak

"The irregular mass of iron and rock entered the outer atmosphere somewhere over eastern Iran, quickly heating up to become a flaming streak across the tranquil summer evening…. The air slowed it, but it was still traveling at a tremendous velocity when it struck Earth at Biskra, near the Tunisian border. In an instant the meteor obliterated the rambling Arabian town. Where forty-six thousand people had lived moments before there was only smoke, a steaming crater whose bottom was a bubbling pool of sand and rock turned into lava, and death."

Excerpt from the novel *Shiva Descending* by Gregory Benford and William Rotsler (Avon, 1980)

Fireball

Twenty seconds after impact, the inhabitants of the east coast of North America become aware that something very frightening has just happened. They are in the streets, wondering why their car or their cell phone has stopped working, when suddenly everything becomes extremely bright and the air turns searingly hot. This is the fireball—a great wave of **thermal radiation** produced by the impact.

Those living in New England, in the United States, and in New Brunswick and Nova Scotia, in Canada, are lucky it is a cloudy evening. The cloud cover reduces the effects of thermal radiation by around 65 percent. But it still feels like a furnace on the streets, and it is not much better inside—the EMP has disabled the air conditioning systems in every building.

The situation is much worse further south: from New York to Florida, and beyond to the Bahamas, Cuba, Haiti, the Dominican Republic, and Puerto Rico, the skies are clear and the heat is intense. It is sufficient to ignite combustible materials, such as trees, grass, litter, and even some clothing. Soon there are mass fires burning, as people run screaming for shelter or shade.

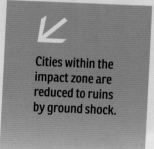

Cities within the impact zone are reduced to ruins by ground shock.

POPIGAI CRATER

Popigai Crater in Siberia, Russia, is 62 miles (100 kilometers) wide, making it the fourth-largest impact crater on Earth. Scientists believe it was created by an asteroid between 3 and 5 miles (5 and 8 kilometers) wide some 35 million years ago. The shock pressure and heat from the impact immediately transformed the graphite in the ground into diamonds within an 8½-mile (13.6-kilometer) radius of the impact site. Today, the area has a number of diamond mines.

The fireball is visible as a bright light in the sky as far away as Miami, Florida; Atlanta, Georgia; and Toronto, in Canada—cities some 1,250 miles (2,000 kilometers) from the blast zone. It lasts for about five minutes, then fades. The fires continue to burn.

Shock waves

The asteroid's impact creates shock waves that travel through the surrounding earth, air, and water. A shock wave in Earth is called **ground shock**; a shock wave in the air is called a **blast wave**; and a shock wave in water is called a water compression wave, which can produce tsunamis. We will now look at the effects of each of these.

Ground shock

When the blast from the impact hits the ocean floor, it sends a wave of energy through Earth that radiates outward in all directions, as well as inward toward Earth's center. Ground shock behaves like an earthquake, and it ripples through Earth's crust at between 4 and 8 miles (6 and 13 kilometers) per second. It hits the east coast a minute after impact, and to the people there, still sweltering under the effects of the fireball, it is like being struck by a powerful earthquake. Buildings topple and giant cracks open up in the road. In New York City, the Brooklyn Bridge, busy with rush-hour traffic, collapses, sending hundreds of cars toppling into the East River. There are also subway tunnel collapses and derailments in several parts of Manhattan, Brooklyn, Queens, and the Bronx. The ground shock is felt as a minor ground vibration as far away as California, South America, West Africa, and western Europe.

The blast wave

The pressure on the air caused by the blast is truly incredible, generating wind speeds of over 1,250 miles (2,000 kilometers) per hour. However, the blast wave rapidly diminishes in energy as it radiates outward. By the time it has traveled 125 miles (200 kilometers), the winds have dropped to about 150 miles (250 kilometers) per hour—enough to sink three ships, including the MS *Limburg*, which was nearby; four commercial airliners are also sent crashing into the sea, with the loss of all on board. By the time the blast wave reaches land, winds are just about 30 miles (50 kilometers) per hour, causing light damage to settlements on the North Carolina coast.

Debris

The asteroid explodes upon impact with the ocean floor. The debris from the asteroid, together with huge amounts of superheated steam (the evaporated sea water) and all the material from the seabed crater, gets ejected into the upper atmosphere. The solid debris is extremely hot— around 9,000 degrees Fahrenheit (5,000 degrees Celsius). Some of the vaporized cloud of rock and dust falls back to Earth within a 1,250-mile (2,000-kilometer) radius of the point of impact. The debris is still very hot, and it ignites mass fires, especially in dry grassland or forested areas.

FACT OR FICTION?

Blast wave approaching...

"George looked up at the sky. It looked fierce and threatening. Colors were swirling. He forced his mind to think. *Five minutes. Five minutes went by between the loss of the TV and the ground shock. That means it is very, very far away*. It is too big to be a nuclear explosion. He raced back to the front of the house and accidentally collided with Debbie.

The ground began to rumble again as a strong aftershock hit. When the motion died down and they got back on their feet, George said:

'That explosion was too far away and too big to be a nuke [nuclear weapon]. Maybe it is an impact.'

'What kind of impact?' Debbie said.

'I'm thinking an asteroid.' George shone the light back into the house.

She said: 'What do we do?'

'There is a large blast wave headed toward us. It might strike in a couple of hours. We need to dig in and dig fast.'"

Excerpt from "Impact Scenario" in the appendix of "Comet and Asteroid Threat Impact Analysis" by James A. Marusek (American Institute of Aeronautics and Astronautics, 2007)

The rest of the ejected material flies further and higher. It quickly spreads around Earth, reaching the other side of the planet over the next few days. In the daylight areas, the debris dims the sunlight. In the nighttime areas, it blots out the Moon and stars. Much of this debris rapidly cools and condenses to form droplets that solidify into tiny glass beads called spherules. Over the next few hours and days, these start to fall back to Earth like light hail. They fall all over the planet's surface.

Superhot material ejected into Earth's atmosphere by the impact strike falls to Earth, sparking bush and forest fires in many parts of rural North America and Central America.

Tsunamis

The asteroid opens up an enormous cavity in the ocean, and water rushes back into it. The sudden movement of such a colossal volume of water causes a ring of tsunamis to radiate outward in all directions from the blast zone. The waves spread through the Atlantic Ocean and the Caribbean. Rather than one big wave, as one sees in movies, the tsunamis form into a series of waves. The average distance between each wave is the same as the diameter of the initial cavity—12 miles (19 kilometers)—and they travel at a speed of around 185 miles (300 kilometers) per hour, leaving an interval of about four minutes between each wave.

WHAT IS A TSUNAMI?

A tsunami is an enormous, powerful wave that can devastate coastal areas. The word *tsunami* is Japanese for "harbor wave," and it is in harbors and other human settlements that its destructive power is truly felt. Tsunamis are caused by a disturbance in the sea that forces a large volume of water to move suddenly. This could be due to an undersea earthquake, volcanic eruption, or landslide—or an asteroid hitting the ocean.

As each tsunami approaches land and the water gets shallower, the wave slows down and grows taller. Moments before the tsunami strikes, the ocean mysteriously recedes. This is the wave pulling the sea into itself. Old shipwrecks and other debris are suddenly revealed on the exposed seabed. In Atlantic City, New Jersey, some locals run onto the wet sand to pick up the flapping, stranded fish. Then a hissing, cracking sound fills the air. They look up and are shocked to see a gigantic wall of water bearing down on them…

The first tsunamis make landfall on the North American coast at 8:15 p.m. EST, two hours after impact. The waves are 330 feet (100 meters) high and they bombard the coast from Cape Cod in Massachusetts to Cape Hatteras in North Carolina, hurling ships onto the land, sweeping away cars, and destroying buildings. New York City, still reeling from the mass fires and the ground shock earthquake, now faces fresh devastation as giant **cataracts** of white water surge through its canyon-like streets, turning them into raging torrents. The death toll runs into thousands as people are drowned, crushed by falling buildings, or hit by cars and buses carried on the flood.

Tsunamis across the Atlantic

By 10:15 p.m., four hours after impact, virtually the entire east coast of North America has been hit by waves 200 feet (60 meters) high or more. Between 9:45 p.m. and 3:45 a.m. the following morning, tsunamis start hitting the exposed shores of the Caribbean and South America. The Bahamas, Cuba, Haiti, the Dominican Republic, and Puerto Rico take the brunt, engulfed by waves of up to 115 feet (35 meters), but they shield a broad region to the south and west, including Colombia and Venezuela. Tsunamis of up to 82 feet (25 meters) bombard the northern coast of Brazil.

The tsunamis reach the eastern limits of the Atlantic Ocean around eight hours after impact. Waves of 50 to 65 feet (15 to 20 meters) strike the fishing towns, beaches, and coastal swamps of West Africa. Many other countries experience major coastal flooding. At about the same time, waves of similar height crash onto the coasts of Spain and Portugal. Nearly five hours later, the tsunamis reach the British Isles. These waves are smaller, having taken a northerly route and been slowed by their passage over the Grand Banks.

The sea recedes from the land just before a tsunami strikes. People on the beach are tempted to wander across the newly exposed sand. Many are caught off guard by the arrival of the tsunami moments later.

Shock and awe

The immediate reaction of people living nearest the blast zone is panic, confusion, and terror, as they are hit by a succession of cataclysmic events. First come the power outages and equipment failures; then the sky turns searingly bright and the temperature soars. Next, burning hot stones and ash start falling out of the sky, setting off fires. Has a nuclear bomb gone off? Has the Sun exploded? People run inside their houses or the nearest building and try to find some relief from the heat and the burning stones. When, seconds later, the ground shock strikes, many people die as walls and ceilings collapse on top of them. In built-up areas, the death and injury toll is horrifically high, as buildings, bridges, and tunnels collapse.

The violence of the ground shock was equivalent to a powerful earthquake. To make matters worse, it struck in an area unaccustomed to earthquakes— the buildings had not been constructed to withstand this kind of natural disaster, and the public and emergency services were unprepared.

Once the ground shock has died away and the stones have stopped falling, dazed survivors tend to their wounds and try to make contact with loved ones. But the phones are still not working. People are desperate to know what has happened, but the few with their own power generators find that televisions and radios are broadcasting nothing but static and the broadband network is down. With no information or way to communicate, people are left on their own, and the instinctive reaction of most is to flee.

People attempt to escape the flooded cities of North America's east coast. They have to abandon their vehicles, which no longer work due to EMP (see page 13).

Water surges between buildings in built-up areas.

Flight to the west

Those on the east coast witnessed the brightness in the sky to the east, so the vast majority decide that their best hope is to head west. Because of the EMP, most vehicles do not work. Motorcycles and scooters are the only kind of motorized transportation that still operate, and there is a desperate scramble for these vehicles. Many are stolen from parking lots or looted from showrooms. However, the vast majority of people leave on foot.

They have barely begun their trek when the first of the tsunamis strikes. The first that most people know of it is a roaring, crashing sound behind them, and then they are knocked off their feet as a frothy white mass of water pours into them. Once again, the death toll is highest in the cities. Here, the foaming waters are forced into narrow channels by the buildings, concentrating their power. As it moves further inland—up to 20 miles (30 kilometers) inland in some places—the surging flood grows clogged with debris, such as cars and bits of building, and these smash into the fleeing population to deadly effect.

WHAT WOULD YOU DO?

Help your country or your family?

As a government scientist living in Washington, D.C., you have figured out what has just happened. You realize that a tsunami is approaching. It is probable that Washington will be flooded. Do you:

(a) try to reach your boss, the Secretary of Homeland Security, to help coordinate a government response to the disaster, or

(b) get yourself and your family to Fort Reno Park, in northwest Washington, the highest—and therefore safest—part of the city?

CHAOS AND PANIC:
THE FIRST FEW DAYS

For those living within about 620 miles (1,000 kilometers) of the impact zone, it seems like the world is coming to an end. In quick succession, they have faced an earthquake, fire, a rain of burning debris, and a tsunami. There are casualties running into the millions. Almost everyone has sustained an injury. For the survivors, it seems as if things cannot get any worse. Little do they know, the disaster is only just beginning…

Dark days

Dawn does not arrive the next morning. All over the world, it is as if the Sun has failed to rise. The upper atmosphere is still choked with debris and is now filling with smoke from the mass fires sparked by the fireball and the superhot falling debris. All the dust and smoke blocks out any sunlight, and for the next three days, the whole world remains dark and cold.

Refugees who managed to escape the flooded cities of the east coast gather on islands of higher ground, such as Bellevue Hill in Boston. Here, survivors huddle around fires to keep warm, scavenging in the streets and in abandoned stores and houses for any food, drink, and medical supplies they can find. Similar scenes can be found on the far side of the Atlantic, where huge crowds of refugees converge on high areas such as Mount Nimba in Guinea.

↗

In the days following the impact, the atmosphere becomes clogged with dust and smoke.

First rescue efforts

Between 12 and 15 hours after impact, communications and electrical power are restored to some areas. Soon afterward, the first rescue helicopters (now returned to service after being disabled by the EMP) arrive in the disaster zones and begin airlifting people to hospitals. They find the hilltops dense with hundreds of thousands of people. The helicopters use searchlights to pick out thousands more, huddled on rooftops or drifting on makeshift rafts through the dirty black waters that swirl through the flooded coastal areas. Even with rescue teams flying in from all parts of the United States, the task is overwhelming. Many of the severely injured die before they can be rescued.

A new seat of government

Among the first refugees to be airlifted to safety are high-ranking members of the U.S. federal government, including the president. With the White House and Capitol Hill flooded, the seat of government is transferred west to the highly secure Cheyenne Mountain Operations Center in Colorado. Once established in its new home, the government begins the process of coordinating rescue efforts, in addition to explaining to the public what has just happened and what actions people should take.

CHEYENNE MOUNTAIN

The Cheyenne Mountain Operations Center (CMOC) is a military installation located about 2,000 feet (600 meters) inside a mountain near Colorado Springs, Colorado. It was built in the 1960s, at the height of the Cold War, as a place where the U.S. government could operate in case of a nuclear attack on Washington, D.C. One of the most secure facilities in the world, it has walls of thick steel plates, 25-ton doors (see below), and reinforced concrete bulkheads. It is designed to withstand a 5-megaton nuclear blast 4 miles (6 kilometers) away. It is one of the few places on Earth that remains immune to the EMP.

Acid rain

Twenty-four hours after impact, the rains come. Thirsty refugees collect the rainwater, but they do not realize that it is deadly. The mass fires have produced poisonous gases, which react with moisture in the air to form clouds of **acid rain**. Over the next three days, the acid rain falls in intense bursts over the eastern United States. It damages plants and trees and pollutes rivers, streams, and lakes. It kills fish and the animals that feed on them or drink the water. Many of those people stranded in the disaster zones suffer painful deaths as they ingest the poisonous chemicals in the water. Others, who understand the science or have been observing its effect, choose not to drink the deadly rain.

Emergency camps

Within a few days, a chain of emergency camps is established just beyond the disaster zone. The entire state of Florida has been declared a disaster zone, so surviving Floridians make their way to camps in the north. These tented communities, gradually replaced during the following months by portable buildings and simple shacks, will become home to millions of refugees for the next few years. Similar camps are built in other parts of the world.

Fumes from the mass fires contain nitrogen and sulfur, which are absorbed by water drops that form clouds, leading to acid rain.

Earthquakes and volcanoes

If the asteroid's effects were limited to the Atlantic coasts, the world might have recovered sooner. Unfortunately, the ground shocks set off earthquakes in some unexpected places. Most travel radially through Earth's crust and decrease in strength the further they go. But some travel downward toward the center of Earth. These shock waves reflect off the planet's solid core and rebound to the surface. The reflected vibrations are powerful enough to set off earthquakes in many of Earth's seismically unstable places.

The ground shocks also awaken the Chaiten Volcano in southern Chile, Mount Vesuvius in Italy, Merapi in Indonesia, and Nyiragongo in the Democratic Republic of the Congo. The world's emergency relief resources, already stretched to the breaking point, must now be directed toward these disasters.

WHAT CAUSES QUAKES AND VOLCANIC ERUPTIONS?

Earth's crust is made up of large pieces called tectonic plates. These plates float on a layer called the mantle, which is made of iron and magnesium-rich rocky material. The places where the tectonic plates meet are called faults. Earthquakes and most volcanic eruptions occur at these faults.

If two plates grind against each other, it can cause an earthquake. If the edge of one plate dives under another into the mantle, or if two plates move apart, volcanoes can form. Eruptions occur when gas in the magma, a very hot semi-liquid rock, forces it up toward the surface. Earthquakes and volcanic eruptions can also be set off by external violent impacts, such as an asteroid.

Effects of the asteroid strike

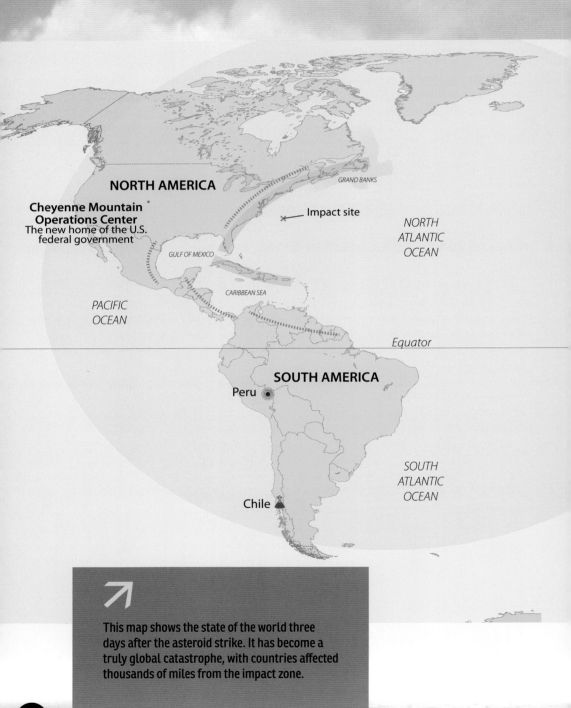

NORTH AMERICA

GRAND BANKS

Cheyenne Mountain Operations Center
The new home of the U.S. federal government

X — Impact site

GULF OF MEXICO

NORTH ATLANTIC OCEAN

PACIFIC OCEAN

CARIBBEAN SEA

Equator

SOUTH AMERICA

Peru

SOUTH ATLANTIC OCEAN

Chile

↗

This map shows the state of the world three days after the asteroid strike. It has become a truly global catastrophe, with countries affected thousands of miles from the impact zone.

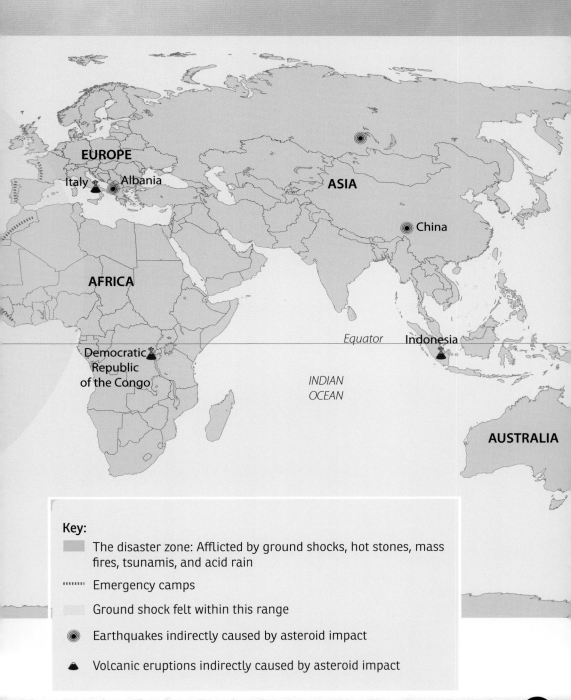

EUROPE

Italy Albania

ASIA

China

AFRICA

Equator Indonesia

Democratic
Republic
of the Congo

INDIAN
OCEAN

AUSTRALIA

Key:

The disaster zone: Afflicted by ground shocks, hot stones, mass
fires, tsunamis, and acid rain

Emergency camps

Ground shock felt within this range

Earthquakes indirectly caused by asteroid impact

Volcanic eruptions indirectly caused by asteroid impact

COLD AND DARK: THE FIRST FEW MONTHS

After three days, sunlight gradually begins to peep through the dense layer of dust, debris, and smoke in the upper atmosphere, but it will be months before the skies are clear. This is mainly due to volcanic eruptions, which ejected vast amounts of ash into the atmosphere, adding to the soot from the mass fires and dust from the asteroid.

Impact winter

The dust and ash take much longer to fall back to Earth than the heavier spherules and hot rocks that fell in the first few hours. They are carried by **jet streams** around the world, so that the dimming of the sky becomes a global event. This is the impact winter, and it lasts until late July 2020. The lack of sunlight also causes plant **photosynthesis** to slow down, so crops fail and animals starve. In the towns and cities, panic buying sets in. In parts of the eastern United States, this descends into rioting and looting. Supermarket shelves soon lie empty. In these violent, chaotic times, the elderly and sick are particularly vulnerable.

During the impact winter, daytime is no brighter than twilight and temperatures plummet.

WHAT IS PHOTOSYNTHESIS?

Plants use sunlight to make energy so they can grow. Their roots absorb water from the ground, and their leaves absorb **carbon dioxide** from the air. They use the sunlight to convert the carbon dioxide and water into sugar, while releasing oxygen as a waste product. The sugar gives the plant energy, enabling it to grow. This process is called photosynthesis, and without it, life on Earth would be impossible.

Rationing

It is days, and in some cases weeks, before governments begin to gain control. In almost every country, a system of rationing is imposed. Each person is given food credits, allowing him or her to purchase a certain amount of a product each month. For example, nursing mothers and children are allowed more than the standard amount of water. Foods that do not need much sunlight, such as cabbage and mushrooms, remain relatively abundant, while sunlight-hungry tomatoes, melons, and peppers disappear altogether.

As the pasture lands die, livestock farmers turn to other sources of food, such as hay and commercially produced animal feed. But soon these supplies also start to run out, and many livestock—particularly in poorer parts of the world—start to die.

HOW LIKELY IS IT?
What are the chances of an impact winter occurring?

The asteroid that struck Earth around 65 million years ago, wiping out the dinosaurs and other species, probably caused a severe impact winter. Evidence from the fossil record and studies of rock layers formed during this time suggest that the impact threw up large amounts of atmospheric dust and sulfuric acid clouds, and this blocked sunlight for around 10 years. More recently, the cold period between 536 and 540 CE, which caused crop failures and widespread starvation, may have been caused by a comet impact.

Powerful volcanic eruptions, releasing large amounts of ash and dust into the atmosphere, can sometimes have a comparable effect. One famous "volcanic winter" occurred after the 1815 eruption of Mount Tambora in Indonesia. As a result of all the ash ejected into the atmosphere, 1816 became known as the "year without a summer." Crop failures in New England, Canada, and parts of Europe caused food prices to rise, leading to riots in Great Britain and France.

Hunger and disease

The several million refugees in the emergency camps, already suffering from shock, grief, homelessness, and injury, now face new threats: cold and hunger. On the Atlantic coasts, the problem of food shortages is especially extreme, because the damage to local road and railroad networks blocks the transportation of food. In many cases, camps are kept supplied by a continuous "air bridge" of helicopters and planes dropping packages of food, warm clothing, and other essentials around the clock.

The camps must also be kept supplied with medicines, as illness and disease spread. Across the disaster zones, the crowded conditions and lack of sanitation in the camps lead to outbreaks of the diseases cholera and typhoid fever. Hundreds of thousands die in this "second catastrophe."

Malnutrition and disease quickly take hold in the refugee camps.

WHAT ARE CHOLERA AND TYPHOID FEVER?

Cholera and typhoid fever are highly infectious diseases that people catch by eating food or drinking water contaminated by human waste. They thrive in crowded conditions such as refugee camps where sanitation is poor. Victims suffer from diarrhea and, if left untreated, can die of **dehydration**.

Community spirit

A spirit of grim determination takes hold of the camp communities. People find ways to adapt to the sudden change in their circumstances. Those with access to computers keep the outside world updated with blogs about life in the camps. They send texts to the rescue helicopters in the flood zones, helping to direct them to places where survivors might be found. Advice is passed around on how to keep warm or trap wild animals for food and fur, and what vegetables can be grown in these sun-starved times.

Social breakdown

Not everyone is so community minded. In some parts of the world, there is a complete breakdown of law and order, and violence and looting become widespread. Gangs quickly form and take control of neighborhoods, forcibly collecting payment from local businesses in return for "keeping order" on the streets. The gangs rule through terror and impose their own form of rationing, helping themselves to the biggest share of what limited resources there are. Many people are forced to beg for food.

The social pressures caused by the disaster are felt most strongly in the cities inland from the disaster zones, such as Philadelphia, Pennsylvania, and Richmond, Virginia (United States), Bogota (Colombia), Kenema (Sierra Leone), Marrakesh (Morocco), Evora (Portugal), and Exeter (United Kingdom). These cities are overwhelmed by refugees from the coasts. Locals become resentful of the newcomers, fearful they will eat all the remaining food. There are violent confrontations, and the governments in these countries vote themselves emergency powers to deal with the crisis. Army units are sent onto the streets, checkpoints are set up, and **curfews** are imposed.

Looting and vandalism happen in many city centers.

31

Popular anger

Public disorder continues, although not all of the anger is directed at refugees. In the weeks following the impact, morale remained surprisingly high, but as the "sunless spring" continues into June, discontent grows. The authorities are criticized for not doing enough. Governments attempt to rally public spirits. The U.S. government adopts the catchphrase "Together we can win!" while the British government attempts to inspire wartime camaraderie by reviving slogans from World War II (1939–1945), such as "Make Do and Mend."

These strategies largely fail, perhaps because, this time, there is no enemy to blame. Major cities are soon filled with the noise of marches and protests that often turn into riots.

Economic crisis

The cost of emergency law enforcement, maintaining prison populations, and running emergency camps places an intolerable burden on the Atlantic nations. Special "asteroid taxes" are levied, but with economic activity so disrupted, hardly anyone is wealthy enough to pay them. Governments try to stimulate their own economies by erecting **trade barriers**.

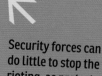
Security forces can do little to stop the rioting, as protestors set fire to stores and businesses.

These force people to buy domestically produced goods, helping local farmers and manufacturers. Soon, governments around the world retaliate with their own **protectionist** measures. The globalized world breaks apart and international trade dries up. Although this gives a short-term boost to home industries, it ultimately leads to a further lowering of living standards, as supplies of imported raw materials grow scarce.

During these harsh times, production of luxury and hi-tech goods is dramatically reduced, as the world's manufacturers focus on supplying people with basics such as clothes, food, medicine, and household items.

The threat of war

The U.S. government's shortage of funds leads it to call in loans from its Latin American neighbors. However, these nations are themselves struggling to absorb all the refugees from the Caribbean, not to mention the cost of emergency care and rebuilding. They refuse to pay. A war of words begins as tensions rise.

On July 20, Mexican border guards open fire on a group of American refugees attempting to cross into Mexico, killing 18 people. When the Mexican government refuses to hand over the border guards, the U.S. government threatens invasion. Both sides mobilize their armed forces and, for a while, war seems inevitable.

Then, on the morning of the seventh day of the crisis, something extraordinary happens: for the first time in nearly four months, the Sun is clearly visible as it rises into the hazy sky. All over the world, people bask in the unexpected warmth and brightness. There are spontaneous street parties celebrating the event. As the days go by, the haze gradually disappears and the sky becomes a glorious blue. The threat of war disappears…

WHAT WOULD YOU DO?

The mayor's dilemma

You are the mayor of a small city faced with starvation and disease, with many neighborhoods under the control of brutal gangs. The government is offering to assist you with troops. Would you:

(a) use the troops to help distribute food and medicine to the needy;

(b) use the troops to break the gangs' stranglehold on your city;

(c) ignore the government offer and pay local gang leaders to help distribute food and medicine in their neighborhoods?

HEAT AND DEADLY LIGHT: THE NEXT FEW YEARS

When the dust finally settles and the skies start to clear in late July 2020, most people see this as the end of the nightmare. A few scientists warn that the celebrations are premature—global temperatures are warmer than they should be—but they are largely ignored.

Within weeks, however, following scientific surveys of land and ocean temperatures and atmospheric gases, people are forced to acknowledge the grim truth: things have not returned to normal. Far from it. Earth has definitely gotten warmer—the average temperature has risen by almost 1.8 degrees Fahrenheit (1 degree Celsius)—and there is also something very wrong with the light.

Global warming

In a United Nations (UN)–commissioned report entitled *Our Post-Impact World*, a team of top climate scientists predict that Earth will go through a period of unusually warm temperatures, possibly lasting years, due to a big increase in the **greenhouse effect**. This has been caused by the enormous carbon dioxide emissions from the volcanoes and mass fires, as well as by the massive ejection of seawater vapor into the atmosphere, following the asteroid strike.

In total, they calculate that around 230 cubic miles (945 cubic kilometers) of ocean water instantly evaporated during the impact. Both carbon dioxide and water vapor are **greenhouse gases**. Unlike ash and dust, however, they will remain in the atmosphere for a long time.

Ultraviolet radiation

All around the world, people are being admitted to hospitals with severe sunburn. The UN report confirms the public's worst fears. Studies show that the **ozone layer**, which protects us from the Sun's ultraviolet (UV) radiation, has virtually disappeared. The damage was done, once again, by seawater vapor, ejected by the asteroid impact into the highest parts of the atmosphere. Chemical compounds in the vapor, such as chloride and bromide, destroyed the ozone. The dust cloud, while it lasted, shielded Earth from the UV light.

Now, with the dust gone, the planet is left fully exposed to the Sun's deadly rays. Just a few minutes of sunlight on bare skin, the scientists warn, is enough to cause sunburn. People with fair skin are especially vulnerable.

WHAT IS THE GREENHOUSE EFFECT?

Most of the Sun's heat is absorbed by Earth's surface, with about one-third of this heat reflecting back toward space. However, certain gases in the atmosphere, such as carbon dioxide, **methane**, and water vapor, trap this reflected heat—similar to the way that glass traps heat in a greenhouse, keeping the greenhouse warm. This process, known as the greenhouse effect, keeps Earth warm and is natural.

However, since the **Industrial Revolution**, things have gotten out of balance. We have consumed vast quantities of fossil fuels—coal, oil, and natural gas—to provide ourselves with heat, power, and transportation. When they burn, fossil fuels give off carbon dioxide, a greenhouse gas. As a result, the amount of carbon dioxide in the atmosphere has greatly increased, trapping more of the Sun's heat and causing global warming.

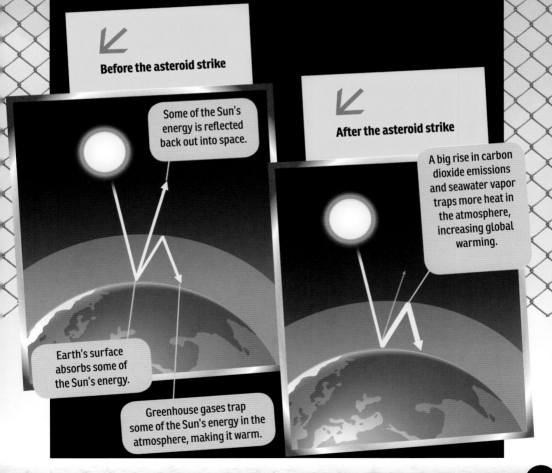

Before the asteroid strike

Some of the Sun's energy is reflected back out into space.

After the asteroid strike

A big rise in carbon dioxide emissions and seawater vapor traps more heat in the atmosphere, increasing global warming.

Earth's surface absorbs some of the Sun's energy.

Greenhouse gases trap some of the Sun's energy in the atmosphere, making it warm.

WHAT IS ULTRAVIOLET LIGHT?

UV light is a type of electromagnetic radiation—energy that travels through space in the form of a wave. Visible light, X-rays, and **infrared** are also forms of electromagnetic radiation, each with their own **wavelength**. The wavelength of UV light is shorter than that of visible light, but longer than that of X-rays. It is called ultraviolet because the wavelength is just a little shorter than that of the color violet, which is the shortest wavelength we can perceive with our eyes. UV light is visible to some insects and birds. It is found in sunlight and causes our skin to tan—and also to burn.

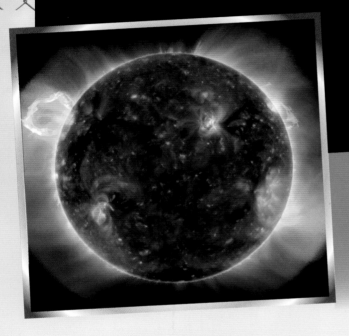

This is a picture of the Sun photographed in UV light. Red areas are relatively cool, while blues and greens are relatively hot.

UV dangers

The ultraviolet index (UVI), the measure of UV radiation, has skyrocketed. Normally, if the UVI reaches 6 or above, it is time to put on sunscreen. Now, for most of inhabited Earth, the UVI is averaging around 20, and in some places it is reaching as high as 56. Scientists reassure people that the ozone layer will repair itself within a couple of years. Until then, people will have to radically change their way of life.

People must try to avoid going outdoors during daylight hours. If they are forced to go out, they should wear sunglasses, a hat, a long-sleeve shirt and pants, and use SPF 30+ sunscreen on exposed skin. Scientists warn people of the consequences of prolonged exposure to UV light, including sunburn, some skin cancers, and damage to the eyes and **immune system**.

People go to great lengths to cover up their skin as much as they can and to use lots of sunscreen.

Adapting to the new conditions

With the days already uncomfortably warm, people need little persuading to adopt a **nocturnal** existence. After the impact winter, many have grown used to the dark anyway. During this era, which becomes known as the ultraviolet spring, businesses adjust their working hours and people adapt to a life of daytime sleep and working nights. The health authorities in many countries issue vitamin D supplements to make up for the loss of sunlight (a crucial source of this vitamin).

Before long, there are thriving new businesses selling UV-resistant outfits, as well as UV-proof tinted windows, curtains, and blinds. Manufacturers of sunglasses and sunscreen can barely keep up with demand. Construction teams create networks of tunnels and sheltered walkways and bridges, so that people can still move around during the day if they need to.

Food supply

Food production is the most challenging problem to be solved. Of course, no crops or livestock can withstand the unfiltered UV light. **Geneticists** experiment with special **enzymes** to make crops UV-resistant. They achieve some success, but only in the most northern and southern climates. For a while, famine looms on an unprecedented scale.

The first to suffer are those most dependent on freshly grown foods, especially isolated rural communities in the developing world. Famine strikes in many of these regions within weeks. People in developed nations—where food supplies can be more easily stockpiled through refrigeration, freezing, canning, and other forms of preservation—are able to shield themselves from the full impact of the catastrophe for several months.

Are plants really damaged by UV light?

Plants obtain energy from sunlight. However, UV light is not absorbed as easily by plants and can actually damage their DNA. To protect themselves, plants have evolved special **pigments** that block UV light. The more UV light there is, the more of these pigments they must produce. This has the effect of changing the plant's cellular structure. It causes the plant's height and leaf size to decrease and makes the plant less green.

Indoor Farms

Meanwhile, around the world, teams of farmers and scientists are already developing a simple yet ingenious solution: indoor farming. By the end of August, construction workers build the first giant prefabricated shed on a farm in Israel. Systems are installed to control light, temperature, humidity, air quality, and nutrition. Initial results are promising and, very soon, similar sheds begin appearing in every part of the world.

All this comes too late to solve the immediate crisis, and as the world's food supply starts drying up, global famine appears inevitable. However, the United Nations Food and Agriculture Organization (FAO) has a plan. It has persuaded world leaders to set aside a portion of their food stocks against the even greater shortages to come. The public, already accustomed to rationing, accepts a further reduction in weekly allowances. As a result, when the world's stores and markets start to run out of food, governments are able to step in and begin supplying universal daily meals.

Each citizen is provided with a packed daily meal.

This is an artist's model of a building that incorporates its own vertical farm. The produce grown on the building can be used to feed the people who live there.

These great efforts by the FAO are undermined, in some countries, by corruption and inefficiency on the ground, as well as violence in areas where governments have lost authority. Many of the sheds are raided by organized gangs. By the time the first crops are harvested from the sheds in early November, it is, sadly, too late for many people.

Nevertheless, the sheds prove highly successful. For the first time in history, farmers are no longer at the mercy of the weather. Crops are grown under consistently ideal conditions. As a result, growth times are shorter, while both quality and yield is high. Many farmers declare they will never go back to the old ways, even when the ozone layer returns.

Ecological impact

While the FAO focuses on the food supply situation, conservation agencies such as the World Wildlife Fund turn their attention to the ecological crisis. The planet's wildlife, already weakened by the impact winter, now faces an even greater threat from the ultraviolet spring. The UV light damages the DNA of animals, causing mutations, cancer, and **cataracts**. It kills plants or suppresses their ability to photosynthesize. Plants are the base of the world's food chain. As they die off, the planet's herbivores (plant-eaters), and then its carnivores (meat-eaters), will also die.

Sulfate haze

The situation appears very bleak, except for one unexpected factor: the sulfate haze. Scientists discover that the volcanic eruptions in Chile, Italy, Indonesia, and the Democratic Republic of the Congo together sent an enormous quantity of sulfur dioxide into the atmosphere. This has formed a haze of sulfate aerosols that is actually working as a kind of ozone replacement, blocking some of the UV radiation. However, a lot of UV light is still getting through—too much for humans to tolerate without getting sick, and enough to wipe out many of the more vulnerable plant and animal species.

Operation Noah's Ark

The scale of the task facing conservationists is overwhelming. No matter what action they take, they know that millions of plants and animals are inevitably going to die. From the beginning, the conservationists agree that their priority must be to save not just individual plants and animals, but rather whole species. That way, the world's **biodiversity** will be preserved and mass extinction will be avoided.

With this in mind, they conceive Operation Noah's Ark. Lists of species are drawn up, starting with the most vulnerable species and the ones unrepresented in zoos and botanical gardens. Insects, burrowing animals, and aquatic animals are left off the list because they will find sanctuary underground or underwater.

Hundreds of thousands of volunteers are recruited from all over the world. They are sent out into a wilderness area near where they live. Equipped with animal-trapping and plant-collecting equipment, they gather up whatever local flora and fauna they can find that is on the list. In theory, a single, healthy specimen of each plant species is all that is required. In the case of animals, two is the bare minimum required—a male and female capable of breeding.

Those animals that can adapt to colder climates are moved south or north of the "UV Lines" (the lines running 50 degrees to the north and south of the equator, beyond which the UV light is more bearable). The rest are placed in sheltered environments. Any large, unused buildings that can be found are refitted as wild animal sanctuaries and plant conservatories.

It is ideal to have two animals of each sex, all of them unrelated, to avoid the problem of inbreeding.

Operation Noah's Ark ends up being expensive and inefficiently run. There are errors in gathering, transporting, and accommodating species. However, after six months, 93 percent of the listed species are saved, and the goal of preserving Earth's biodiversity is more or less achieved. As a bonus, many new species are discovered. At the same time, conservationists sadly acknowledge that many more that have never been identified are now lost forever.

Stepping back into the day

By the fall of 2022, scientists declare that the ozone layer has restored itself and it is now safe for people to venture outside during daylight hours. But many choose not to, because the days remain uncomfortably warm and people have grown used to their nocturnal existence.

HOW LIKELY IS IT?

Could humans become nocturnal?

Humans, like most animals, are governed by an internal clock called our circadian rhythms. These determine when we sleep and when we wake. The clock runs on a 24-hour cycle and is affected by signals from the environment—light and dark being the main ones. When it is dark, our circadian rhythms release a **hormone** called melatonin, which makes us sleepy. Sometimes, our circadian rhythms get disrupted—for example, when we get jet lag. Many people, such as night-shift workers and airline pilots, must adjust their circadian rhythms to do their jobs. It is possible to adapt to a more nocturnal lifestyle, although some research suggests that, over a long period, this can take a toll on a person's health.

Tough times

The decades that follow are harsh. Global warming leads to a dramatic melting of glaciers and sea ice and a rise in sea levels, swamping many low-lying islands and coastlines. There are heat waves, droughts, extreme weather events, and a spread of deserts. Many of the species that were saved by Operation Noah's Ark do not survive their return to the wild.

For humanity, the asteroid strike and its effects leave a scar that will take generations to heal. Around 100 million people died in the catastrophe and its aftermath, and vast numbers of survivors must live with crippling injuries. Earth has become a frightening realm of high temperatures and violent weather. By contrast, the pre-impact days seem like a lost age of peace, comfort, and prosperity.

Economic productivity is a mere fraction of what it was back then. There are energy shortages, housing shortages, water shortages, and hospital bed shortages. It is 20 years before the last disaster zone refugees are finally able to move into permanent homes. By then, the community spirit of the early months of the crisis is a distant memory. The public has grown sick of endless **austerity**. Politicians and their promises are largely distrusted.

↖

Many people chose to abandon society altogether in order to try to fend for themselves.

And yet...

And yet the legacy of the asteroid strike is not entirely negative. The indoor farming experiment revolutionizes food production. Rationing ends in most countries by 2023, and by 2035, for the first time in human history, hunger is eliminated as a major issue of global concern.

Thanks also to the asteroid, humankind finally manages to break its addiction to fossil fuels and a pattern of consumption that is depleting the world so rapidly of essential resources. The grim, daily reality of global warming is enough to convince almost everyone that pumping more carbon dioxide into the atmosphere is no longer a viable option. Before long, every house has its own solar panel or wind turbine, and the roads fill up with hydrogen-powered vehicles. The new energies are expensive, unreliable, and prone to run out at inconvenient moments—but then life in this post-impact world was never going to be easy!

WHAT CAN WE DO?

What can we do to avoid the awful events described in the previous chapters? The first and most important thing to do is to keep watching the sky. In the scenario depicted in this book, there was no warning: a gigantic space rock came out of nowhere and slammed into the Atlantic. In reality, we must hope that we would get some notice before such an event.

Hunting for asteroids

The dinosaurs never saw their asteroid coming. The chances are that we will be better prepared. Since 1998, the U.S. government's **National Aeronautics and Space Administration (NASA)** has been scanning the heavens for near-Earth objects (NEOs). These are asteroids, comets, and other objects with orbits that bring them close to Earth.

The goal of NASA's Spaceguard Survey is to identify and track the motion of all NEOs bigger than half a mile (1 kilometer) in diameter. In May 2012, NASA announced that it had identified and tracked 934 NEOs of this size (843 asteroids and 91 comets). This represented 95 percent of the total number estimated to exist (981). Of the asteroids found so far, 152 have orbits that might possibly bring them into collision with Earth, but none presents a threat within the next 100 years. As for the comets, they have much longer orbits and are more difficult to track, but scientists estimate that they are 100 times less likely than asteroids to make a close approach to Earth—which is why the focus has been on asteroids.

NASA has also been tracking mid-sized NEOs, ranging from about 330 feet (100 meters) to half a mile (1 kilometer) in size. So far, 5,200 out of an estimated 19,500 have been found and tracked, and 993 have orbits that could one day pose a threat to Earth.

GROUND-BASED ASTEROID TRACKING

Most asteroid discoveries are made using Earth-based telescopes. Asteroids are found by obtaining a number of photographs of the same region of sky. Computers then analyze these photos to identify any objects that appear to "jump" between the stars. These may be an asteroid or other orbiting body. Further work is then required to distinguish "main belt" asteroids that orbit between Mars and Jupiter from NEOs.

In addition to the work being done by NASA, many others are also involved in the hunt for asteroids. The European Space Agency (ESA) runs a Space Situational Awareness Preparatory Program, with a mission to watch out for and provide information on space hazards, including potential asteroid impacts. The ESA is being helped in its search by many amateur astronomers, who have the patience and expertise to help track down NEOs.

Scientists are getting better and better at predicting the future **trajectories** of asteroids. This is good news for us, since it means we should get plenty of warning of a collision. Jon Giorgini, a senior engineer at NASA's Jet Propulsion Laboratory, says: "We're showing that searches with optical telescopes and follow-up observations with radar telescopes can provide us centuries of advance notice about potential close encounters of asteroids with Earth."

Currently, our biggest threat comes from an asteroid called Asteroid 1950 DA, which has a diameter of half a mile (1 kilometer). There is a small chance that it will hit Earth on March 16, 2880. According to Jon Giorgini:

"How close 1950 DA will approach Earth turns out to depend on the asteroid's physical attributes—its size, shape, and mass, and how it spins, reflects light, and radiates heat into space. These things are unlikely to be known any time soon."

The Spaceguard Center and Observatory in Wales, in the United Kingdom, plays its part in the international effort to detect and observe NEOs.

Avoiding the asteroid

Assuming we do get some warning of an approaching asteroid, what then? Scientists believe we could devise a technique to prevent a collision. There is disagreement about how best to achieve this. Some argue that the best strategy would be to deflect the asteroid from its path, so that it misses Earth. Others believe that destroying the asteroid would be the only safe option.

Deflection and destruction

One method of deflecting an asteroid might be to detonate nuclear weapons some distance away, knocking it off course. Another option would be to send up a heavy, unmanned spacecraft to hover near the asteroid. The gravity exerted by the spacecraft would hopefully, over time, pull the asteroid into a non-threatening orbit. Another method is the use of a giant lens to focus solar energy on the asteroid's surface. The resulting vaporization of material would, if all goes according to plan, push it in a different direction.

A powerful nuclear bomb detonated a few hundred feet away from the asteroid could be enough to shatter it into small fragments. However, the fragments might then continue on a collision course with Earth. Multiple small impacts could prove just as destructive as a single large impact.

Regardless of which method scientists settle on, some experts suggest that we should start work on the project right now. As David Morrison of NASA's Ames Research Center asks: "Why wait until we're really at risk to develop the technology to deflect it?" Astronaut Ed Lu adds: "The first attempt to deflect an asteroid should not be when it counts for real, because there are no doubt many surprises in store as we learn how to manipulate asteroids."

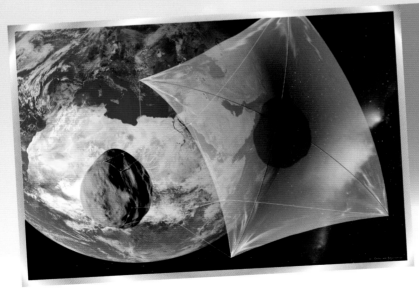

In the future, a sunlight-powered solar sail could pull an asteroid out of its collision course with Earth.

FACT OR FICTION?

Bombing the comet

"President Beck: We watched as the bombs shattered the second comet into a million pieces of ice and rock that burned harmlessly in our atmosphere and lit up the sky for an hour."

From the movie *Deep Impact* (1998)

Keeping watch

We know, from our studies of space and of Earth's long history, that from time to time our planet will be struck by large rocks. Asteroid strikes may be very rare, but they are as natural and inevitable as earthquakes and volcanoes. However, unlike an earthquake or a volcano, this is one kind of natural disaster we may be able to prevent. If we are to do so, we must never stop keeping watch over the skies.

WHAT WOULD YOU DO?

The president's decision

You are the Russian president. A giant asteroid is heading for Earth, estimated to strike near St. Petersburg. The city will be completely wiped out. However, there is a slim chance that a secret space mission will manage to deflect it using focused solar energy. There is no time now for an organized evacuation from the city. Do you:

(a) keep the information secret to avoid a general panic, hoping that the mission will succeed;

(b) announce the threat to the public and tell people to get out of the city as fast as they can;

(c) organize the secret evacuation of people who will be useful in the coming national and global emergency: health professionals, engineers, scientists, soldiers, and government officials?

A final word...

In the immortal words of *The Hitchhiker's Guide to the Galaxy*: DON'T PANIC! Please do not let this book give you nightmares. Remember, an asteroid might hit Earth only once every 600,000 years or so, and this is very, very unlikely to happen any time soon.

WRITE YOUR OWN STORY

Why not write your own story about an asteroid strike? It is a great subject for fiction. You could certainly grab your readers' attention with descriptions of the collision and all the terrible disasters that would inevitably follow. But just because the subject matter is exciting, that does not mean your story is guaranteed to succeed. Writing fiction is a craft that needs to be worked at. Here are a few basic tips to get you started.

Plan

It is really important to plan your story before you start writing it. Otherwise, you might find you have gotten halfway through and you have no idea how to continue it. The plan should be a summary of what you want the story to be about and should include your ideas about the characters, the setting, and the plot. Remember, the great thing about the plan is that you do not have to stick to it. Once you start writing, you may think of other, better ideas, and that's great—follow your instincts!

Characters

Who is going to be your main character? Do you want it to be someone at the center of the action, like a political leader or scientist, or just an ordinary person caught up in the crisis? To make your character come alive, it is often a good idea to give him or her some sort of quirk or trait. This might then become significant, in some unexpected way, during the story. She may be a computer geek who hacks into NASA and learns about a secret space mission to divert an asteroid, for example. Or he may be a non-swimmer who loves his cat, which he ends up having to rescue from a flood following a tsunami.

Think also about the other main characters. For a short story, you do not want too many characters, or you will end up confusing the reader and possibly yourself. Even though you are going to write about an epic, world-shaking event, it is usually best to limit yourself to about three or four main characters and focus on their experience of the crisis.

Setting

Next, decide on the setting. When and where do you want to set your story? If you want your story to include a space mission to deflect or destroy the asteroid, it would be best to set it in the future, since we do not have these techniques yet. Think about what technologies might be available. How have everyday activities such as eating and dressing changed? Adding in this sort of detail can help your story to come alive.

Plot

Finally, you need to think about the plot. What actually happens in your story? You do not have to be too detailed at this stage. But you do need to figure out the basic sequence of events, including the ending. When plotting, it is worth thinking about dramatic tension—how will you keep your readers turning the pages? In an asteroid strike scenario, you may want to make the strike itself the climax. The dramatic tension could come from not knowing whether the rock will hit Earth, or whether a last-ditch space mission can deflect it. Or you could open the story with the strike (it would make for a spectacular opening!), and the dramatic tension could then come from not knowing whether your hero or heroine will survive.

That is about it for your preparation. But before you start to work on your story, you might want to do a bit of research. Check out pages 54–55 for some good books and web sites. Slipping in a bit of factual information here and there always helps to give a story credibility.

Good luck!

TIMELINE

APRIL 6, 2020

6:15 p.m. EST
(Eastern Standard Time, the time zone that includes the eastern parts of the United States and Canada)

An asteroid enters the atmosphere, creating a brief, bright flash of ultraviolet light

6:16 p.m. EST
The asteroid explodes as it hits the Atlantic Ocean east of the U.S. coast. An electromagnetic pulse caused by the explosion knocks out all electric power within 1,250 miles (2,500 kilometers). Ionizing radiation from the blast interrupts the world's communications.

6:16–6:21 p.m. EST
The fireball from the explosion causes a surge in temperature and sparks fires across North America's eastern seaboard

6:17 p.m. EST
The ground shock from the impact hits North America's east coast, causing a violent earthquake

6:30 p.m. EST
Red-hot debris starts falling from the sky, igniting mass fires in some places within 1,250 miles (2,000 kilometers) of the impact zone

7:12 p.m. EST
Debris from the blast has spread around the world, blocking out the sunlight in daylight areas. Spherules begin falling around this time and continue falling for the next few days.

8:15 p.m. EST
The first tsunami makes landfall on the North American coast. More tsunamis follow about once every four minutes, gradually diminishing in strength and frequency over the next few hours.

9:45 p.m. EST
Tsunamis start striking the Caribbean and South America. They reach West Africa and western Europe around eight hours after impact.

APRIL 6-8, 2020

Ground shocks from the asteroid impact set off volcanoes in Chile, Italy, Indonesia, and the Democratic Republic of the Congo and earthquakes in Albania, China, Russia, and Peru

APRIL 7, 2020

With the atmosphere clogged with debris, the following day is as dark as night—it is the start of the impact winter. Refugees from disaster zones gather on higher ground. Rescues begin. Acid rains start to fall.

APRIL 8-15, 2020

The U.S. government re-establishes itself in the Cheyenne Mountain Operations Center in Colorado. Emergency camps are set up outside the disaster zones on both sides of the Atlantic.

APRIL 9, 2020

From this time, the days become a little less dark, but the light is still very dim from all the dust and ash

MID-APRIL 2020

Panic buying begins as stores begin to run out of food

MAY 2020

Systems of rationing are introduced. "Air bridges" are established to keep the emergency camps supplied with food, warm clothing, and so on. There are outbreaks of disease in some camps.

JUNE 2020

Law and order break down in many towns and cities close to the Atlantic coasts, which have become overwhelmed by refugees. Army units are sent onto the streets to try to prevent riots and looting. Prison populations grow. Governments raise trade barriers and global trade collapses. In many countries, there are shortages of essentials such as oil, gas, sugar, and rubber.

JULY 20-25, 2020

Tensions between the United States and Mexico seem certain to lead to war

JULY 26, 2020

The skies suddenly clear; it is the end of the impact winter. All over the world, people celebrate.

AUGUST 2020

The temperature is uncomfortably warm and sunburn cases skyrocket. A UN report says that the asteroid strike has caused a dramatic increase in global warming and also wrecked the ozone layer, exposing the world to UV light. Governments warn people to stay indoors. People change to a nocturnal lifestyle—the start of the ultraviolet spring.

AUGUST 2020-JANUARY 2021

Operation Noah's Ark saves thousands of vulnerable wild animal and plant species from UV radiation

AUGUST 2020-MARCH 2021

The FAO coordinates with charities and governments to provide universal daily meals for everyone when stocks start to run out

SEPTEMBER 2020-APRIL 2021

Giant sheds for indoor farming are built over farms around the world. First crops are harvested in November and are declared a great success.

SEPTEMBER 2022

The ozone layer is repaired. The ultraviolet spring is officially over, and it is safe to go out in daylight.

2023

An indoor farming revolution helps to end rationing in most countries

2040

Earth's climate finally stabilizes and temperatures fall to more comfortable levels

GLOSSARY

acid rain rainfall made acidic by atmospheric pollution, so that it causes harm to the environment

austerity difficult economic conditions caused by government cuts to public spending

biodiversity variety of life in the world or in a particular habitat

blast wave destructive wave of highly compressed air spreading outward from an explosion

carbon dioxide gas that is given off when fossil fuels, such as coal, oil, and natural gas, are burned. It is called a greenhouse gas because it traps heat from the Sun in Earth's atmosphere and adds to the greenhouse effect.

cataract (1) sudden rush of water

cataract (2) medical condition in which the lens of the eye becomes less transparent, leading to blurred vision

curfew regulation requiring people to remain indoors between certain hours

dehydration condition of having lost a large amount of water from the body

Eastern Standard Time time in the zone that includes the eastern states of the United States and parts of Canada

electric current flow of electricity

electromagnetic pulse (EMP) intense pulse of electromagnetic radiation, usually generated by a powerful explosion and occurring high above Earth's surface

electromagnetic radiation kind of energy, in the form of waves, that includes visible light, radio waves, X-rays, infrared, and ultraviolet light

enzyme substance produced by a living organism that increases the rates of chemical reactions in the organism

extraterrestrial not from Earth

flash blindness temporary blindness caused by exposure to a light flash of extremely high intensity

geneticist scientist specializing in the science of genetics, the study of how organisms inherit characteristics

greenhouse effect trapping of the Sun's warmth by gases in Earth's atmosphere

greenhouse gas gases such as carbon dioxide and methane that trap the Sun's warmth

ground shock shockwaves that travel through Earth, caused by an explosion or sudden, violent movement in the ground

hormone chemical released by a cell or gland that sends out messages to other cells in the body. Hormones regulate functions such as digestion, growth, and mood.

immune system organs and processes of the body that provide resistance to infection

Industrial Revolution rapid development of industry in some parts of the world during the late 18th and 19th centuries, brought about by the introduction of machinery, steam power, and the growth of factories

infrared form of electromagnetic radiation with a wavelength just greater than that of the red end of the visible light spectrum

ionizing radiation type of radiation (such as X-rays or gamma rays) with enough energy to cause ionization (stripping atoms or molecules of their electrons)

jet streams narrow band of very strong air currents encircling the globe dozen of miles above Earth

megaton unit of explosive power equivalent to one million tons of the explosive called TNT

meteor streak of light in the sky caused by a meteoroid entering the atmosphere

meteorite debris of a meteoroid that survives its passage through the atmosphere and hits Earth's surface

meteoroid small body of up to 33 feet (10 meters) in diameter that moves through the solar system

methane colorless, odorless flammable gas

National Aeronautics and Space Administration (NASA) agency of the U.S. government that is responsible for the nation's space program

nocturnal of the night

ozone layer layer in Earth's atmosphere, around 12 to 18 miles (20 to 30 kilometers) from the surface, containing a high concentration of the gas ozone

photosynthesis process by which plants use sunlight to create energy from carbon dioxide and water

pigment natural coloring matter of animal or plant tissue

protectionist describing a policy that protects a country's domestic industries from foreign competition by raising trade barriers

thermal radiation heat energy

TNT high explosive

trade barrier government restriction on imports. This could be in the form of tariffs (taxes on imports) or embargoes (banning imports).

trajectory path followed by a flying object

wavelength distance between successive crests of a wave

FIND OUT MORE

Nonfiction

Atkinson, Stuart. *Comets, Asteroids, and Meteors* (Astronaut Travel Guides). Chicago: Raintree, 2013.

Owen, Ruth. *Asteroids and the Asteroid Belt* (Explore Outer Space). New York: Windmill, 2013.

Fiction

Johnstone, Michael. *Asteroid Strike* (Future Tense). New York: Franklin Watts, 2000.

Raphael, Elaine, and Don Bolognese. *Asteroids Alert* (2050: Voyage of the Starseeker). New York: Scholastic, 2000.

Web sites

airandspace.si.edu/etp/asteroids
The web site of the Smithsonian National Air and Space Museum is full of fascinating information about asteroids.

www.impact.arc.nasa.gov
The NASA Ames Research Center looks at asteroid and comet impact hazards.

www.nasa.gov/mission_pages/WISE/news/wise20120516.html
This section of the official NASA web site gives up-to-date news about the search for NEOs.

science.nationalgeographic.com/science/space/solar-system/asteroids-comets-article/
Learn more about asteroids on this National Geographic web site.

Movies

Armageddon (1998, rated PG-13)
This science-fiction drama is about a space mission sent by NASA to stop a huge asteroid on a collision course with Earth.

Asteroid (1997, not rated)
In this science-fiction drama, Earth is hit by asteroids.

Deep Impact (1998, rated PG-13)
This science-fiction drama describes the attempts to prepare for and destroy a 7-mile- (11-kilometer-) wide comet headed for Earth.

National Geographic: Asteroids—Deadly Impact (2003, not rated)
This documentary explores the history and future possibilities of asteroid strikes.

Topics to research

1. Investigate an existing asteroid impact crater. Find out its size and age. What was Earth like at the time of the impact? How might the asteroid have affected life on the planet?

2. Imagine you have been asked to design a family home for a post-impact world. What are some of the factors you would have to keep in mind? How would it be different from the homes we are used to today?

3. Research the techniques astronomers use to spot NEOs. Go to solarsystem.nasa.gov/multimedia/video-view.cfm?Vid_ID=2522 to see a video of an asteroid in motion.

INDEX